D1601598

# *Nita Mehta's*
# Vegetarian
# SandwicheS

## 100% TRIED & TESTED RECIPES

**Vegetarian**

## *Nita Mehta*

B.Sc. (Home Science), M.Sc. (Food and Nutrition) Gold Medalist

## Tanya Mehta

**SNAB**

PUBLISHERS PVT LTD

*Nita Mehta's*
## Vegetarian
## SandwicheS

First Edition 2005
ISBN 81-7869-087-x

*Food Styling and Photography:* **SNAB**

*Layout and laser typesetting :*

National Information
Technology Academy
3A/3, Asaf Ali Road
New Delhi-110002
☎ 23252948

*Published by :*

**SNAB**
**Publishers Pvt. Ltd.**
3A/3 Asaf Ali Road,
New Delhi - 110002
Tel: 23252948, 23250091
Telefax:91-11-23250091

*Editorial and Marketing office:*
E-159, Greater Kailash-II, N.Delhi-48
*Fax:* 91-11-29225218, 29229558
*Tel:* 91-11-29214011, 29218727, 29218574
*E-Mail:* nitamehta@email.com
snab@snabindia.com
*Website:* http://www.nitamehta.com
*Website:* http://www.snabindia.com

*Distributed by :*

THE VARIETY BOOK DEPOT
A.V.G. Bhavan, M 3 Con Circus,
New Delhi - 110 001
Tel : 23417175, 23412567; Fax : 23415335
Email: varietybookdepot@rediffmail.com

*Printed by :*

AJANTA OFFSET & PACKAGING LTD

**Rs. 89/-**

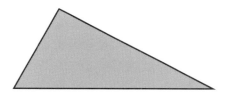

# Introduction

Sandwiches are no longer tea-time treats. With different kinds of breads available and more so, because of whole wheat and other healthy options of bread, sandwiches make a complete, well balanced meal. We have used vegetables, processed cheese or paneer, beans, natural herbs to make the sandwiches healthy and delicious at the same time. The fresh, light and innovative recipes are surely going to be appreciated by all your family members. These days, the range of sandwiches is really huge. You'll have a choice for each of your family member, be it a child, an adult or an older person.

You can choose from pan grilled to toasted sandwiches to sandwiches for children or the low cal sandwiches. The latest subway sandwiches are also included in this book. All recipes are delicious and quick to prepare.

In the beginning of the book we have given a few tips which one must go through for perfect results. Every recipe is tried and tested and guaranteed to satisfy you.

*Nita Mehta*

ABOUT THE RECIPES

WHAT'S IN A CUP?

**INDIAN CUP**
**1 teacup = 200 ml liquid**
**AMERICAN CUP**
**1 cup = 240 ml liquid (8 oz.)**
**The recipes in this book were tested with the Indian teacup which holds 200 ml liquid.**

# CONTENTS

## Pan Crisp and Toasted Sandwiches   13

# Latest Sub Sandwiches 55

# Sandwiches For Children 68

# Open Sandwiches   82

# Low Cal Sandwiches   93

# Some Sandwich Accompaniments   101

# Spreads for Sandwiches

*Put any one of these spreads on slices of French bread loaf or any ordinary bread and have it grilled or just as it is! You can put any combination of vegetables on it and then grill or keep in the oven at 200°C for 12-15 minutes till crisp.*

**Garlic Spread -** Mix 8 crushed flakes of garlic (1 tsp) with 6 tbsp softened butter. Add 2 tsp lemon juice and a pinch of salt.

**Mustard Spread -** Mix 2 tsp mustard paste, 1 tsp dried herbs, 1 tsp lemon juice, pinch of salt and pepper with 6 tbsp softened butter.

**Coriander Cumin Spread -** Mix 1 tbsp finely chopped fresh coriander, 1 tsp lemon juice, 1 tsp coarsely ground cumin (jeera), salt and black pepper with 6 tbsp softened butter.

**Herb & Mushroom Spread -** Blend 2 tsp dried herbs, 1 cube grated cheddar cheese, 2-3 chopped mushrooms together in a mixer to a paste. Mix this paste with 6 tbsp softened butter and use.

**Honey Cheese Spread -** 3 tbsp salted butter (soft), 2 tbsp cheese spread (plain), 1 tsp honey, ½ tsp pepper. Mix all ingredients together.

# Poodina Chutney

½ cup chopped poodina (mint) leaves, 1 cup chopped hara dhania (coriander)
1 onion - chopped, 2 green chillies - chopped
1½ tsp amchoor, 1½ tsp sugar, ½ tsp salt

1. Wash hara dhania (coriander) and mint leaves.
2. Grind all ingredients with just enough water to get the right consistency of the chutney.

# Eggless Mayonnaise

3 tbsp oil, 2 tbsp flour (maida)
½ cup cold milk, 1 tsp lemon juice
50 gm (¼ cup) cream, ½ tsp mustard powder
1 tsp powdered sugar, ¼ tsp salt, ¼ tsp pepper powder

1. Heat oil in a small heavy bottomed pan. Add flour. Reduce flame and stir for a minute. Add milk, stirring continuously. Boil. Cook till a thick white sauce is ready.
2. Whip white sauce after it cools to room temperature. Add lemon juice, salt, mustard powder, pepper and sugar.
3. Gently mix in cream. Keep in the fridge till serving time.

# Tips about Sandwiches

- To grill sandwiches, remove all metal plates from the oven, except the wire grill (jaali). Preheat oven to maximum temperature with the top and bottom heating rods 'ON'. Butter the sandwich on the outer side also (both sides) with softened butter and place on the wire grill or wire rack for 5-7 minutes or till crisp.
- Use different breads for variety - brown bread, spice bread, milk bread, as well as buns or rolls for a wider selection of sandwiches.
- Keep a ready-made bottle of mayonnaise in the fridge. It is very handy.
- Soften butter or margarine for easy, economical spreading.
- Avoid having too much filling or topping- it makes the sandwich untidy.
- If the filling contains too much moisture, apply it just before serving or lay a lettuce leaf on the buttered bread before applying the filling.
- 500 gm softened butter will spread 80 slices if 1 tsp is used per slice.
- Wrap sandwiches without cutting the sides, in foil or in a damp napkin to keep them supple and fresh. Cut the crust only at the time of serving to prevent the edges from drying.
- Use a sharp knife preferably with a saw edge for cutting sandwiches. Cut sandwiches into interesting shapes.

# Pan Crisp & Toasted Sandwiches

any pan crisp sandwich can be toasted on the grill or in the sandwich toaster instead of making it crisp on the pan. Also any toasted sandwich can be cooked on a pan. It entirely depends on your own choice.

# Paneer Tikka Sandwich

*Picture on cover*                    *Serves 4*

200 gm paneer - cut into small pieces (chopped), 1 small capsicum - chopped
4 slices of bread - lightly buttered

**MARINADE**

½ cup dahi (curd) - hang in a muslin cloth for 15 minutes
½ tsp bhuna jeera powder (roasted cumin powder), ½ tsp red chilli powder
½ tsp chaat masala, ½ tsp salt, or to taste
½ tsp haldi, ½ tsp garam masala, ½ tsp dhania powder
1 tsp ginger garlic paste (8-10 flakes of garlic and 1" piece of ginger - crushed)

1. Hang dahi (curd) in a muslin cloth for 15 minutes.
2. Mix all ingredients of marinade in a bowl. Mix well. Add paneer and capsicum. Keep aside for 15 minutes.
3. Heat 1 tbsp oil in a pan, add marinated paneer & capsicum. Cook on low heat for 5-6 minutes or till dry & golden brown from some sides.
4. Sprinkle ¼ tsp each of bhuna jeera, salt, garam masala and dhania powder on the cooked paneer. Mix. Remove from fire.
5. On each lightly buttered bread, spread some paneer tikka mixture.
6. Cover with another slice. Press gently. Toast in a pan in 1 tsp oil till golden brown from both sides. Cut into two triangles.

# Pickled Sandwiches

*Serves 2*

4 large slices of bread - spread lightly with butter
2 cheese slices or grate 2 cheese cubes
½ tsp peppercorns (saboot kali mirch) - crushed

**MIX TOGETHER IN A BOWL & KEEP ASIDE FOR 10 MINUTES**

1 kheera (cucumber) - peeled & scraped with a peeler to get paper thin long pieces
1 thick green chilli - cut lengthwise, remove seeds and chop finely
¼ cup white vinegar
¼ cup hot water, 1 tsp salt, 1 tsp sugar

1. Mix all ingredients written under mix together. Strain after 10 minutes.
2. On the unbuttered side of a bread, arrange pickled kheera (cucumber) slices and a little green chilli so as to cover the whole slice.
3. Spread grated cheese or a keep a cheese slice on the cucumber.
4. Sprinkle some pepper. Cover with another buttered bread slice, keeping the buttered side on outside. Press. Place the prepared sandwich on the wire rack of a hot oven at about 220°C till golden on both sides.

# Marinated Pesto Sandwich

*Picture on page 1*                    *Serves 3*

a small slab of mozzarella cheese (75-80 gms) or paneer
1 tbsp balsamic vinegar or 1 tsp lemon juice + ¼ tsp sugar
½ tsp oregano, a pinch of salt
2 tomatoes - sliced thinly
6 slices of bread (use regular bread or garlic bread loaf or any other bread loaf)
some salt to sprinkle

## PESTO SAUCE
1½ cups basil leaves or fresh coriander
¼ cup pinenuts (nyoze, chilgoze) or walnuts - toasted in a kadhai or oven till
light brown
2 flakes garlic - roughly chopped
¼ cup parmesan cheese or any processed cheese - grated
4 tbsp olive oil, or any cooking oil
½ tsp salt, ¼ tsp fresh pepper corns (saboot kali mirch)

1. Cut the cheese block into thin slices (about 6).
2. In a flat bowl mix balsamic vinegar or lemon juice with sugar, oregano

and a pinch of salt. Add the mozzarella slices or paneer. Mix well turning sides so that all the sides get coated with the balsamic vinegar marinade.

2. Dry roast the pinenuts in a non stick pan or in a kadhai till they turn light golden. *If using walnuts, there is no need to roast them.*

3. Put basil, nuts, garlic, cheese, salt and peppercorns in a mixer and grind to a paste.

4. With the motor still running, add the oil in a steady stream until well combined.

5. Store the pesto in the fridge in a bottle. Pour some olive oil in the bottle, over the top, to prevent the basil from turning brown.

6. Spread 1¼ tsp pesto sauce on all the slices. Put 2 slices of marinated cheese on it. Place 4 slices of tomatoes. Sprinkle salt and pepper. Press the second slice on it, keeping the pesto side inside. Cut into 2 pieces from the middle. Serve as it is or grill till crisp.

**Note:** You can use ready-made Pesto sauce also. Spread 1 tsp of it on each slice.

# Falafel Pockets

*I have used pita bread for this recipe. You can substitute it with pizza base also, if pita bread is unavailable.*

*Picture on facing page*          *Serves 2*

1 pita bread or 1 pizza base
2½ cups kabuli channa (safed chhole)
2 onions - finely chopped
1-2 tsp garlic - finely chopped
2 tsp green coriander - finely chopped
½ tsp dhania powder (ground coriander)
½ tsp jeera (cumin) powder, 1 tsp salt
1 tsp soda bi carb (mitha soda), oil for frying
½ cup bread crumbs
some onion rings sprinkled with chat masala
some mayonnaise or cheese spread

1. Soak channas for 6-8 hours. Drain and grind in a grinder to a paste.
2. Add finely chopped onions, garlic, coriander leaves, dhania powder, jeera powder, salt and soda-bi-carb. Mix very well.
3. Keep the mixture for 4-5 hours or overnight in the fridge.

4. Make round patties about 1½" in diameter, roll in bread crumbs.
5. Heat oil and fry (kebabs), 1 to 2 at a time, on medium heat till golden brown. Keep aside.

6. Cut the pita bread or pizza base into 2 pieces.
7. Open a piece with a knife from the cut side, going almost till the curved edge, keeping the base joint from the edges, such that you get a pocket.
8. Heat a pan on fire. Saute these pieces till light golden on both sides.
9. With the help of a knife, open to form a pocket, spread some mayonnaise or cheese spread inside the pocket. Throw some onions sprinkled with chat masala inside the pockets. Push 2-3 hot falafel tikkis in it. Warm on a hot tawa for 1-2 minutes. Serve hot with hummus or ketchup.

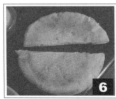
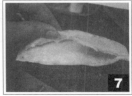
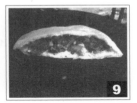

◄ *Club Sandwich : Recipe on page 22*

# Club Sandwich

*A three layered toasted sandwich.*

*Picture on page 20*                    *Serves 2-3*

50 gms paneer- cut into thin slices
1 cheese slice
1 small cucumber (kheera)- wash & slice along with the peel into paper thin slices
6 slices of white or brown bread
some butter - enough to spread

**MIX TOGETHER IN A BOWL**
4 tbsp mayonnaise (use ready-made or see page 11)
¼ cup finely chopped capsicum (simla mirch)
¼ cup finely shredded cabbage (band gobhi)
¼ cup grated carrot (gajar)
¼ tsp pepper, ½ tsp mustard paste

1. Mix mayonnaise, capsicum, cabbage, carrot, pepper and mustard paste in a bowl. Mix well. Check seasonings. Add more if required.
2. Slice paneer into thin slices and sprinkle salt and pepper on it.
3. Toast all the bread slices and spread some butter on one side of each bread. Place a cheese slice. Lay some cucumber slices on the cheese. Place another buttered toast on it, with the butter side down on the cucumber pieces.
4. Place a paneer slice on the bread. Spread some mayonnaise mixture on the last slice of bread and press on the paneer slice. Keep this sandwich aside.
5. Repeat with the other slices to make another sandwich.
6. Trim the edges of a sandwich and cut each sandwich diagonally into four pieces. Serve sandwich with french fries and tomato ketchup.
7. To decorate the sandwich, pierce a small piece of lettuce or cabbage leaf through a tooth pick and top with a cherry or grape or an olive.

**Variation:**

You can also use a thin vegetable cutlet instead of the paneer slice.

# Sliced Potato Sandwiches

*Toasted bread sandwiched with sauted slices of potatoes, paneer & cabbage leaves.*

*Makes 8 sandwiches*

250 gms paneer (cottage cheese)
2 big potatoes - boiled & sliced
8 cabbage leaves (take 1 small cabbage) - each leaf torn into 3-4 pieces
3-4 firm tomatoes - cut into slices, salt and pepper to taste
some mayonnaise or cheese spread - enough to spread
8 bread slices, 3-4 tbsp butter

1. Cut paneer and potatoes into thin slices.
2. Heat 2 tbsp butter in a big nonstick pan. Put few slices of potato on it and then shift to the sides. Turn when the under side is light brown. Put more slices in the centre and brown them.
3. Repeat with all other potato slices. Let them be on the sides of the pan.

4. Put some more butter. Saute the paneer slightly. Shift to the sides.
5. Place the cabbage leaves also on the hot pan. Saute till black patches appear on few sides of the leaves. Remove from heat. Leave everything in the pan.
6. Lightly toast the bread slices. Spread cheese spread on one side and some butter on the other side of 4 slices.
7. On each toast place some cabbage leaves on the cheese spread.
8. Cover the leaves with 2-3 potato slices. Sprinkle salt and pepper. Put paneer slices over the potatoes. Put tomato slices over the paneer.
9. Cover with another toasted slice, keeping the buttered side on the outside. Press gently. Keep aside till serving time.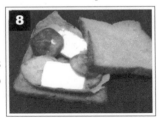
10. To serve, heat on the pan till the bread turns crisp. Cut into 2 halves and serve with tomato ketchup or mustard sauce.

# **Herbed Tomatoes on Bread**

*Hot & crisp garlic flavoured bread pieces topped with herbed tomatoes.*

*Makes 20 pieces*

### TOPPING
2 tomatoes - pulp removed and chopped finely
2 tbsp mozzarella or pizza cheese - cut into ¼" cubes, 1¼ tsp chopped garlic
1 tbsp fresh basil leaves - chopped (tender tulsi leaves may be used)
½ tsp dried oregano, 2-3 tbsp olive oil, ½ tsp salt, ½ tsp pepper

### BREAD
a French bread - cut into slices of ½" thickness, about 18-20 slices
4 tbsp olive oil, 2-3 flakes garlic - crushed

1. Cut each tomato into 4 pieces and gently remove all the seeds and pulp. Chop the deseeded tomatoes into very small pieces.
2. Mix all the other ingredients of the topping with chopped tomatoes and keep aside at room temperature for at least 30 minutes for the tomatoes to absorb the flavours.
3. For the bread, mix 2-3 crushed garlic flakes with 4 tbsp olive oil.

4. Spoon ¼ tsp of this flavoured oil on each slice and spread it on the slice with the back of the spoon. Keep aside till serving time.
5. At serving time, bake the bread slices in a pre-heated oven at 200°C/360°F for 10 minutes till each is lightly toasted and crisp. Alternately, toast the slices on a pan or tawa on low heat till crisp at the bottom.
6. Spread 1 heaped tbsp of tomato mixture (at room temperature) on the toasted slice. Serve immediately.

# Herbed Mushrooms on Bread

200 gm mushrooms - chopped finely, ¾ cup chopped fresh parsley or coriander
1 big onion - chopped very finely, 4 flakes garlic - chopped very finely
¾ tsp salt,½ tsp freshly ground peppercorns, or to taste, 1 tsp dried oregano

1. Heat 4 tbsp oil. Add onions and garlic. Cook for 2 minutes till onions turn light brown.
2. Add mushrooms and cook for 2-3 minutes. Add parsley or coriander.
3. Add salt, pepper and oregano and mix well. Remove from fire.
4. Use it on garlic bread instead of the tomato mixture. Proceed from step 3 of the above recipe.

# Lebanese Smoked Sandwich

*Picture on facing page*                    *Serves 2- 3*

2 Lebanese bread or pita bread or pizza base
75 gms paneer - cut into 1" rectangular pieces of ½" thickness (¾ cup pieces)
1 capsicum, 125 gm big mushrooms (4-5), 1 tomato
½ tsp freshly crushed pepper, ½ tsp oregano, ¾ tsp salt

### MIX TOGETHER
3 tbsp cheese spread, 2 tsp curd

1. Wash capsicum, mushrooms and tomato. Pat dry on a clean cloth. Rub melted butter on them all over. Insert a fork or a knife on to the greased capsicum. Roast on a naked flame, turning sides, directly on the heat till charred (slightly blackened) from various sides. Roast for 2-3 minutes. Cool. Chop the smoked capsicum. Roast the mushrooms and tomato also in the same way on a naked flame. Chop both finely.

*Contd...*

2. Roast paneer also in the same way on the naked flame with forks or tongs. To hasten the process you can use 4 forks on the same flame at the same time.
3. Mix all the smoked ingredients together in a bowl. Add pepper, oregano and ¼ tsp salt. Mix well.
4. Mix together cheese spread and curd in a small bowl. Keep aside.
5. Open up the Lebanese bread from one side, like a pocket. On each pita bread or Lebanese bread spread inside the bread ½ of the cheese spread and curd mixture. Spread on just one side.
6. Spread ½ of the smoked vegetable mixture on the curd mixture.
7. Keep on a hot pan or tawa and cook for about 2-3 minutes on both sides. Cut into four triangle pieces. Serve.

◁ *Chilli Paneer Footlongs : Recipe on page 32*

# Chilli Paneer Footlongs

*Picture on page 30*                    *Serves 8*

1 loaf long French bread, some butter to spread
100 gm pizza or mozzarella cheese - grated
1 spring onion - chopped along with greens or ½ capsicum - diced
a few fresh red chillies or tomato slices - for garnish
2½ tbsp maida (flour)

**TOMATO SPREAD**
6-8 flakes garlic - crushed
¼ tsp red chilli paste - (soak 3-4 dry red chillies in some warm water and grind
to a smooth paste in a mixer with 4 tbsp water)
½ cup ready made tomato puree, 2 tbsp tomato sauce
1 tsp oregano (dried), ½ tsp salt and ¼ tsp pepper, or to taste

**CHILLI PANEER**
100 gms paneer - cut into ¼" cubes, ½ tbsp soya sauce, ½ tbsp vinegar
¼ tsp salt and ¼ tsp pepper, ½ tsp red chilli flakes
½ tsp garlic paste (3-4 garlic flakes - crushed)

1. Marinate paneer with all the ingredients given under chilli paneer for 2 hours.
2. Sprinkle maida on the paneer. Mix gently to coat. Deep fry in 2 batches till golden brown.
3. To prepare the tomato spread, heat 2 tbsp oil. Add garlic and cook till light brown. Add all the other ingredients and cook on low flame till thick. Keep aside.
4. To assemble, cut the loaf into two length ways. Butter each piece on the cut surface and the sides. Grill till crisp and light golden.
5. Spread some tomato puree, sprinkle some grated cheese and then spread the fried chilli paneer.
6. Top with some spring onions or diced capsicum and red chillies. Grate some more cheese.
7. Grill till cheese melts. Cut into 4 pieces and serve.

**Note:** You could fry some boiled and cubed potatoes and use instead of paneer.

# Corn Vegetable Sandwich

*Serves 5*

10 slices bread - spread with a little butter
¾ cup corn kernels (tinned or freshly boiled) or ¾ cup finely chopped carrot
½ capsicum - cut into half rings
2 tbsp butter
1 onion - cut into half and then into half circles
¼ tsp haldi (turmeric powder)
1 tsp ginger paste (½ " piece of ginger - crushed to a paste)
2 boiled potatoes - mashed roughly
½ tsp salt, or to taste
¼ tsp pepper, or to taste
2 tsp tomato sauce
½ tsp soya sauce
5 tbsp grated cheese (use tin or cubes)

1. Heat 1½ tbsp butter. Add onion and cook till golden brown.
2. Add ¼ tsp haldi. Stir. Add ginger paste. Mix. Add potatoes and stir fry for 1 minute on low heat. Add salt, pepper, tomato sauce and soya sauce.
3. Mix well. Add corn or carrot. Saute for 1 minute. Add capsicum. Remove from fire.
4. Take a slice, spread 1 tsp butter on one side. Then spread 2 tbsp vegetable filling on it. Sprinkle 1 tbsp grated cheese on the corn filling. Cover with another buttered slice. Press.
5. Heat your sandwich toaster or the oven to 200°C. Place the grill in the center of the oven. Place the sandwiches on the grill or in the sandwich toaster and grill for 10 minutes or till the sandwiches are crisp and golden. Cut into 2 triangular pieces and serve hot with ketchup.

**Note:** You can also pan fry the sandwiches. Heat a pan or tawa with 1-2 tsp oil. Place the sandwich in the pan and pan fry. Cook the sandwich till well browned and crisp on both sides.

# Grilled Mushroom Toasts

*Servings 8*

4 slices bread - toasted
50 gms mushrooms - chopped
1 tiny onion - chopped finely
3 tbsp butter, 2 tbsp maida (plain flour), ¾ cup milk, salt, pepper to taste

**TOPPING**
25 gms cheese - grated (3 tbsp), 1 tomato, coriander leaves

1. Heat 3 tbsp butter in a pan. Add onion & mushrooms. Cook for 3-4 minutes.
2. Add maida and cook for 1 minute on low flame. Remove from fire.
3. Add milk, stirring continuously. Cook on fire until a thick paste is ready.
4. Remove from fire. Add salt and pepper to taste.
5. Cut each toast into 4 triangles. Apply this mixture on each piece.
6. Grate cheese over them. Garnish with a tomato slice and coriander.
7. Grill for 5 minutes in a hot oven until light brown. Serve immediately.

# Hot Lemon Bread

*Serves 8*

*1 French loaf or loaf of garlic bread.*

**LEMON FLAVOURED BUTTER**
6 tbsp butter - softened, rind of ½ lemon
1 tbsp lemon juice, a pinch salt
¼ tsp freshly ground black peppercorns (saboot kali mirch)

1. Slice the loaf into ½" thick slices, leaving the loaf attached at the bottom.

2. To prepare the lemon butter grate a firm lemon very gently on the fine sides of a grater to get lemon rind. Mix butter with lemon rind, juice, salt and pepper.
3. Spread the butter inside each slit and little over the top.
4. Wrap the loaf in an aluminium foil and keep aside.
5. To serve, bake in a preheated oven at 200°C for 15-20 minutes.
6. Open the foil for the last 5 minutes to make the top crisp.

# Minty Corn 'n' Pea Hot Dogs

*Picture on facing page*          *Serves 4*

5 hot dog buns (long buns), ¾ cups curd - hang for 15 minutes in a muslin cloth
½ cup peas (matar)
¾ cup tinned corn kernels (bhutte ke daane)
1 firm tomato - remove pulp and cut into thin long pieces
¼ cup grated cheddar cheese (use tin or cubes)
salt & pepper to taste

### GRIND TOGETHER TO A GREEN PASTE
¼ cup poodina (mint), ¼ of an onion, 1 small flake of garlic
¼ tsp kala namak (black salt), ¼ tsp bhuna jeera (roasted cumin powder)
½ tsp salt to taste, 1 tsp oil, ¼ tsp pepper, ¼ tsp sugar

1. Hang curd in a muslin cloth for 15 minutes. Keep aside.
2. Grind all ingredients written under grind together to a paste.
3. Beat hung curd well till smooth.
4. To the hung curd, add the green paste, mix.

*Contd...*

5. Add corn and peas to the green paste. Mix well.
6. Heat 2-3 tbsp butter on a tawa or a non stick pan.
7. Divide the bun into two halves with a knife.

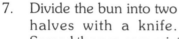

Spread the pea corn mixture on the bottom piece of the base and top with tomato slices.
8. Sprinkle cheese on the tomato. Top with the second piece of bun.
9. Heat the buns on a non stick pan in 1 tbsp oil and cook till crisp OR heat an oven to 180°C and grill the buns for 8-10 minutes or till crisp.

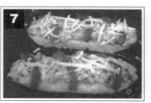
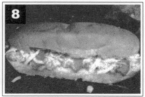

◁ *Double Duet Sandwiches : Recipe on page 42*

# Double Duet Sandwiches

*Double Duet means like a double filling (2 TIER) sandwich. Sufficiently sustaining for a light meal. A few ready-made potato chips can be served along with these sandwiches to make the meal wholesome.*

*Picture on page 40*                    *Serves 2*

3 white bread slices, 6 brown bread slices
14-15 paalak leaves - steam by placing them in a big steel strainer kept upon a pan of boiling water for 2 minutes, till leaves turn a little soft
3 tbsp grated cheese (1 cube)

**YOGURT SPREAD**
1 cup curd - hang for ½ hour
50 gm paneer - grated or ½ cup home made paneer - mashed
½ tsp salt
½ tsp black or white pepper
½ tsp bhuna jeera (roasted cumin powder)
½ tsp mustard powder
1 tsp red chilli sauce or tomato sauce

## VEGETABLES (MIX TOGETHER)
½ cucumber - peeled, grated (½ cup), 1 small carrot - finely grated (½ cup)
1 tomato - cut into 4 pieces, remove pulp and chop
¼ tsp salt, 2 pinches pepper, or to taste

1. Tie the curd in a muslin cloth and hang for 30 minutes.
2. Mix grated vegetables, tomato, salt and pepper. Mix well.
3. Beat hung curd till smooth. Add paneer, salt, pepper, bhuna jeera and mustard powder and chilli sauce or tomato sauce. Keep aside.
4. Spread 1 heaped tbsp curd paste on one slice of brown bread.
5. Cover with paalak leaves. Spread 1/3 portion of the vegetables.
6. Top with a buttered white slice with buttered side down. Press lightly.
7. Spread 1 tbsp curd spread again on this slice. Sprinkle 1 tbsp cheese.
8. Top with a buttered brown slice with the buttered side down. Press.
9. Keep aside. Similarly make 2 more sandwiches. Wrap them in a cling film and refrigerate.
10. At serving time, remove the side crusts and cut into half diagonally to get 2 triangular 2 tier sandwiches from each.

# Sesame Triangles or Rounds

*Servings 12*

6 bread slices
2½ tbsp olive oil
1 small onion - chopped finely
1 carrot - chopped finely (diced)
1 capsicum - chopped finely (diced)
1 potato - boiled and grated
½ tsp tabasco sauce
1 tsp vinegar
½ tsp pepper
¼ tsp red chilli powder
salt to taste
sesame seeds (til) - to sprinkle
chilli garlic tomato sauce to dot

1. Heat 1½ tbsp olive oil. Add onions. Cook till transparent.
2. Add carrot and capsicum. Cook for 3-4 minutes on low flame.
3. Add potatoes, tabasco, vinegar, salt, pepper and chilli powder. Cook for 2-3 minutes. Keep aside.
4. Cut the bread into 2 triangular pieces or cut with a sharp lid or a cookie cutter into rounds. Spread some olive oil lightly on both sides of all the pieces.
5. Spread some potato mixture on the bread pieces. Press. Sprinkle sesame seeds. Press. Grill till bread turns crisp from the under side. Serve, dotted with chilli-garlic sauce.

# Pan Crisp Paneer Sandwich

*Makes 8*

8 slices brown bread, butter - just enough to spread
some shredded carrot and cabbage, to garnish

**FILLING**
100 gm paneer - mashed roughly
1 capsicum - very finely diced, 2 tsp tomato ketchup
2 green chillies - deseeded and chopped very finely
5-6 saboot kali mirch (pepper corns) - crushed roughly
salt to taste, 1 tsp softened butter

1. Mix all ingredients of the filling together. Add enough salt as it tastes bland otherwise.
2. Butter the slices. Spread a layer of the filling on the unbuttered side and press the second slice on it, keeping the buttered side out side.
3. Heat a non stick tawa or pan. Put the sandwiches on it. Press with a potato masher to make them crisp. Turn sides to brown both sides.
4. Serve sprinkled with some shredded carrots and cabbage.

# Cheesy Spinach Toasties

*Serves 4-5*                    *Picture on page 58*

1½ tbsp butter, 4 slices bread
2-3 flakes garlic - crushed (½ tsp)
100 gm (25-30) leaves of paalak (spinach) - washed & shredded
1½ cups grated paneer (150 gm)
5 tbsp grated mozzarella or pizza cheese, 1 tbsp chopped coriander
¼ tsp salt and pepper or taste, ½ tsp red chilli flakes

1. Wash and shred spinach leaves into thin ribbons.
2. Heat butter in a kadhai. Add garlic and stir. Add spinach and cook till all the moisture of the spinach evaporates. Remove from heat.
3. Mix together - grated paneer, coriander and 4 tbsp grated mozzarella cheese, leaving behind 1 tbsp for the topping.
4. Add cooked spinach to the paneer and mix well. Add salt and pepper.
5. Toast the slices and spread the mixture on the toasts. Sprinkle some mozzarella cheese. Sprinkle some red chilli flakes too.
6. Heat in an oven at 210°C for 2-3 minutes. Cut each slice into 4-8 triangles.

# **Mango Chutney Submarine**

*Serves 4-5*

1 long garlic bread - cut lengthwise to get 2 thin long pieces
1 tbsp butter - softened
2 tbsp ready-made sweet mango chutney (fun food)

## TOPPING

1 kheera (cucumber) - cut into round slices without peeling
2 firm tomatoes - cut into round slices
250 gm paneer - cut into 1½" squares of ¼" thickness
few poodina (mint) leaves to garnish - dipped in chilled water
1 tbsp oil

## SPRINKLE ON PANEER

¼ tsp haldi (turmeric powder)
½ tsp red chilli powder
½ tsp salt
1 tsp chaat masala

1. Spread butter on the cut surface of both the pieces of garlic bread.
2. Place the garlic breads in the oven at 200°C on a wire rack for 10-12 minutes till crisp and light brown on the cut surface. Keep aside.
3. Cut paneer into ¼" thick, big square pieces.
4. Sprinkle the paneer on both sides with some chilli powder, salt, haldi and chaat masala.
5. At serving time, heat 1 tbsp oil in a non stick pan. Saute paneer pieces on both sides in oil till slightly toasted to a nice yellowish-brown colour. Keep aside.
6. To assemble the submarine, apply 1 tbsp mango chutney on each garlic bread.
7. Sprinkle some chaat masala on the kheera and tomato pieces. Sprinkle some chat masala on the paneer also.
8. Place a piece of paneer at an angle, then kheera, then tomato and keep repeating all three in the same sequence so as to cover the loaf. Keep paneer, kheera and tomato, slightly overlapping. Insert fresh mint leaves in between the paneer and vegetables, so that they show. Serve.

**Note:** Mango chutney is easily available in bottles in stores.

# Nutty Spinach Slices

*Nutty sesame seeds on toasts.*

*Serves 4-5*

10-12 diagonally cut slices of a French loaf
or
6 slices of white or brown bread
2 tbsp butter
1 tsp crushed garlic

**TOPPING**
salt & pepper to taste
1 tbsp butter
1 tsp lemon juice
4 (50 gm) mushrooms - cut into thin slices
2 cups shredded spinach (200 gm)
2 tbsp til (sesame seeds)
50 gm (2 cubes) cheese - grated

1. Heat oven at 210°C.
2. Make garlic butter by mixing butter and garlic and apply on the bread. Grill for 7 minutes till crisp (you can also toast on a non stick tawa.)
3. Meanwhile prepare the topping. Heat 1 tbsp butter in a non stick pan or a kadhai and add mushroom slices. Saute for ½ minute and remove to a plate.
4. Heat the left over butter in the same pan. Add sesame seeds (til) and wait for 1 minute or till the seeds change colour. Add the spinach and cook till water evaporates. Add ¼ tsp each of salt and pepper. Add lemon juice and mix well. Remove from heat.
5. Spread spinach on toasted bread, spoon some mushrooms and top with grated cheese.
6. Grill for 2-3 minutes at 210°C at serving time. Cut into squares if using ordinary bread or serve whole slices if French bread slices have been used. Serve hot.

# Panzerotti

*An excellent Italian kind of sandwich. Fresh dough is prepared, filled with a filling and deep fried.*

*Gives 20*

## DOUGH

2-3 tbsp lukewarm water, ¼ tsp sugar
1 tsp heaped dried yeast (5 gms)
½ teacup milk, 1 tbsp refined oil, ¾ tsp salt, ½ tsp sugar
150 gms (1½ packed cups) maida (plain flour)

## FILLING

2 tbsp oil
1½ cups finely sliced baby corns
3½ cups finely chopped spinach
1 tsp salt, 1 tsp pepper, ½ tsp red chilli flakes
2 pinches grated nutmeg (jaiphal)
¾-1 cup grated cheese (75 gm)
oil for frying

1. For the dough, mix warm water and sugar in a cup. Feel the water with a finger to check if it is lukewarm. Add yeast. Shake the cup gently to mix the yeast. Cover it and leave it in a warm place till the granules of the yeast disappear and it becomes frothy. (10-15 minutes). (If it does not swell, discard it).

2. Mix milk, oil, salt and sugar in a pan. Keep aside. When the yeast becomes frothy, heat this milk mixture to make it lukewarm. Add the ready yeast mix to the lukewarm milk mixture.

3. Add this yeast and milk mixture to the maida and knead well to make a smooth dough. Grease a big polythene, brush the dough with a little oil and put it in the polythene. Keep it covered in a warm place to swell for 1 hour or till it is double in size. Now punch it down to its original size, brush with oil and keep it back in the polythene for another 15 minutes or till it swells again.

4. For the filling, heat oil. Add baby corns and fry till it changes colour. Add spinach and mix for 1 minute. Add salt, pepper, red chilli flakes and nutmeg.

*Contd...*

5. Cook till the mixture is dry and the babycorns are tender. Remove from fire to a bowl.
6. Mix in grated cheese.
7. Divide dough in 20 marble sized balls. Take one and roll out into a 3-4" round thin chappati using dry flour for dusting.
8. Place a little filling in the centre of the chappati, leaving sufficient border all around for sealing the edges.
9. Brush the edges with water. Fold over and press together to seal. Keep in the fridge till serving time.
10. At the time of serving, deep fry 3-4 at a time, on moderate heat, until golden. Drain on a paper napkin and serve immediately with chilli-garlic sauce.

**Note:** You can have any filling of your choice. The size can also be varied as per your liking.

# Latest Sub Sandwiches

## Serve your sandwich in style...

- To decorate the sandwich, pierce a small piece of lettuce or cabbage leaf through a toothpick and top with a cherry or a grape. Insert the toothpick on the sandwich.
- Serve them with French fries (see page 101) or just with boiled vegetables sauted in olive oil/butter, oregano, salt and pepper.

# Potato Croquettes Subwich

*Picture on facing page*     *Serves 2-3*

1 loaf french bread (9"), 1 small onion - sliced, ½ cup shredded lettuce

### CROQUETTE (POTATO SEEKH)
1 small onion - finely chopped, 2 tbsp butter
2 small carrots - grated (1 cup), 1 cup grated cauliflower
2 potatoes - boiled & grated, 2 tsp cornflour, 1 tbsp tomato ketchup
1 tsp salt or to taste, ¼ tsp pepper

### COATING
2 tbsp cornflour mixed with ¼ cup water, ½ cup dry maida (flour)
¼ tsp each of salt, ¼ tsp pepper

### MIX TOGETHER
¼ cup grated cabbage, 2½ tbsp ready-made mayonnaise
2 tsp milk, ¼ tsp lemon juice, a pinch of salt and pepper

1. For the croquettes, heat butter in a pan. Add onion. Cook for 2-3 min.
2. Add carrots and cauliflower, cook for 4-5 minutes.
3. Mix boiled and grated potatoes. Add cornflour, tomato ketchup, salt and pepper. Mix well and cook for 6-7 minutes.
4. Remove from fire and let the mixture cool down. Shape into long rolls (seekhs) about 2½" in length.
5. Dip the seekhs in a thin cornflour batter and immediately roll over dry cornflour also spread in a plate. Keep aside in the refrigerator to set.
6. Shallow fry croquettes in oil in a pan till crisp.
7. Make a slit in the French loaf going till the end, but let the end be intact. Cut it into 3 pieces.
8. Spread lettuce and onion on each piece.
9. Arrange 2 croquettes on one side of the bread.
10. Spread the mayonnaise mixture on the croquettes. Sprinkle salt and pepper.
11. Heat 1 tbsp oil in a pan and put the sub in a pan and cook till crisp from both sides. Serve hot.

◁ *Cheesy Spinach Toasties : Recipe on page 47*

# Romance

*Picture on page 103*                    *Serves 2*

1 loaf french bread
½ of a small red capsicum - chopped
½ of a green capsicum - chopped, 1 tomato- deseeded and chopped
1 onion- chopped,  3-4 jalapenos or 1 green chilli - chopped
2 cheese slices or 4 tbsp grated cheese, salt and pepper to taste

**MINTY HONEY MUSTARD DRESSING (MIX TOGETHER IN A BOWL)**
2 tbsp honey, 3 tbsp chopped mint (poodina), 1 tbsp olive oil
1 tbsp mayonnaise, 2 tbsp mustard, ½ tsp garlic, a pinch of salt

1. Cut the loaf into 2 pieces lengthwise.
2. Arrange a cheese slice or grated cheese on the base of the loaf.
3. Spread red capsicum, green capsicum, tomato, onion and jalapeno.
4. Spread the minty honey dressing on top of veggies. Sprinkle salt and pepper. Cover with the other piece of loaf.
5. Cut loaf into two pieces from the middle. Serve as it is or warm in a microwave for just 30 seconds or on a tawa for 2 minutes. Serve immediately.

# Sweet Onion Sub

*Serves 2*

1 loaf French bread, 1 cup shredded lettuce or cabbage
1 capsicum- sliced, 1 tomato - sliced, salt and pepper to taste

**ONION DRESSING**

4 tsp butter, ½ tsp garlic paste, 1 onion - sliced, 1 tsp sugar, 2 tsp white wine
½ tsp soya sauce, 2½ tbsp water

1. Heat butter in a pan, add garlic paste. Add onion and sugar, cook till onion turns soft.
2. Add wine, soya sauce and water. Mix well and cook for 1 minute. Remove from fire.
3. Make a slit in the French loaf going till the end, lengthwise.
4. Spread 1 cup shredded lettuce on the base of the loaf.
5. Arrange capsicum and tomato slices.
6. Cover with the prepared dressing on top. Sprinkle salt and pepper.
7. Press the top portion lightly. Cut sub into two pieces from the middle to get 2 small pieces. Warm on a pan for 1-2 minutes or just heat in a microwave for just 30 seconds.

# Greek Pizza Pockets

*Serves 3-4*

½ cup ready-made mayonnaise or see page 11
2 Lebanese breads or 2 pizza bases
1 cup peas (matar)
1 cup grated potato
1 tbsp butter, ¾ tsp salt, ½ tsp pepper, ¼ tsp oregano
1 cup cornflakes - roughly crushed
4- 5 lettuce leaves or ½ cup shredded cabbage
1 tbsp curd, ½ tsp salt, ¼ tsp pepper
1 small onion - cut into rings, 2 small tomatoes - deseeded and sliced

1. Heat 1 tbsp butter, add matar and cook for 2-3 minutes.
2. Add grated potato and cook for 2-3 minutes. Remove from fire.
3. Add salt, pepper, oregano and 1 cup roughly crushed cornflakes. Mix.
4. Let it cool. Churn the cooled mixture in a mixer to a smooth paste.
5. Make 8 balls with the mixture. Deep fry in hot oil till golden. Let it cool. Press the balls in between palms to get a flattened shape.

6. Open up the Lebanese bread or pizza base from one side by cutting with the knife, like a pocket. On each pita bread or Lebanese bread, spread inside the bread 1½ tbsp mayonnaise. Sprinkle onion rings. Arrange 4 pressed balls. Spread tomato and lettuce leaves. Sprinkle salt and pepper.
7. Keep on a hot pan or tawa and cook for 2-3 minutes on both sides. Cut into 4 triangular pieces and serve.

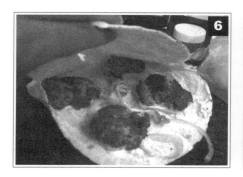
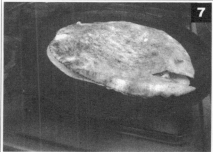

# **Fusion Special**

*Serves 2*

1 loaf French bread (9")
100 gms paneer (cottage cheese) - cut into ¼ " square pieces
½ of a green capsicum- diced
1 tomato - deseeded and chopped
1 onion - chopped
1 tbsp chopped cilantro or coriander
2 cheese slices - cut each into 2 triangular pieces
salt and pepper to taste
4 tbsp shredded lettuce or cabbage

## **CREAMY BBQ DRESSING**

3 tbsp tomato ketchup, 2 dry red chillies, 4 tbsp water
1 tsp soya sauce, ½ tsp vinegar, ½ tsp chopped garlic, a pinch of salt
1 tsp worcestershire sauce, 1 tsp mustard sauce
a few drops of tabasco sauce, 2 tbsp cream
½ tsp brown sugar (optional), 2-3 peppercorns (saboot kali mirch)
1 laung (cloves), ¼" stick dalchini (cinnamon), ½ tsp saunf (fennel)

1. Churn all ingredients of BBQ dressing in a mixer to a smooth paste.
2. Marinate paneer, capsicum, tomato, onion and coriander with the BBQ dressing, keep aside for ½ hour.
3. Make a slit in French loaf going till the end. Arrange a cheese slice or grated cheese on the base of the loaf.
4. Spread the marinated veggies. Sprinkle salt, pepper and shredded lettuce or cabbage. Cover with the top piece.
5. Cut loaf into two 6" pieces. Serve as it is or warm in a microwave for just 30 seconds. Serve immediately.

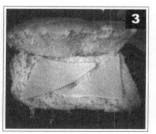

# Indiana Jones

*Picture on inside front cover*     *Serves 2*

1 loaf French bread (9")
1 onion - chopped, ½ tsp garlic paste
2 potatoes - boiled and chopped
1 tomato - deseeded and chopped
5- 6 slices of pickled cucumber (use ready-made or see page 102)
½ cup cabbage or lettuce leaves - shredded
2 tbsp butter
salt and pepper to taste

**BBQ DRESSING**
2 tbsp tomato ketchup, 2 dry red chillies, 4 tbsp water
1 tsp soya sauce, ½ tsp vinegar, ½ tsp chopped garlic, a pinch of salt
1 tsp worcestershire sauce, 1 tsp mustard sauce
a few drops of tabasco sauce
½ tsp brown sugar (optional), 2-3 peppercorns (saboot kali mirch)
1 laung (cloves), ¼" stick dalchini (cinnamon), ½ tsp saunf (fennel)

1. Churn all ingredients of BBQ dressing in a mixer to a smooth paste.
2. Melt butter in pan, add onion, cook till soft, add garlic, mix well.
3. Add potatoes and cook for 5- 6 minutes, till golden from various sides.

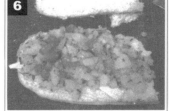
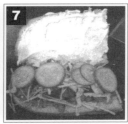

4. Add salt, and pepper. Remove from fire.
5. Make a slit in French loaf going till the end.
6. Spread the potato pieces on the base of the loaf.
7. Spread the tomato, pickled cucumber and cabbage.
8. Spread 3 tbsp of the dressing on top of veggies. Sprinkle salt & pepper.
9. Cut loaf into two pieces. Serve as it is or warm in a microwave for just 30 seconds. Serve immediately.

Sandwiches For Children

# Spinach Pizza Margherita

*Pizza is spread with a healthy spinach tomato sauce. Children love this.*

*Makes 2 pizzas*

2 pizza bases or 4 bread slices
2 tbsp oil, 1½ cups chopped palak, ¾ cup readymade tomato puree
½ tsp salt, ¼ tsp pepper, ½ tsp oregano, ½ tsp sugar
1 tbsp tomato sauce, 1½ cups grated mozzarella or pizza cheese

1. Heat oil in a pan, add chopped spinach, cook for 3- 4 minutes.
2. Add readymade tomato puree, salt, pepper, oregano, sugar and tomato sauce. Cook for 3- 4 minutes. Remove sauce from fire.
3. Spread 1 tbsp melted butter or olive oil over each pizza base, covering the edges.
4. Spoon some spinach tomato sauce over pizza base.
5. Sprinkle ½ cup mozzarella cheese on each base. Sprinkle some salt, pepper and oregano to taste. Drizzle some olive oil on the cheese.
6. Place on the wire rack of the oven (not tray) and bake at 200°C for 12-15 minutes or until the base turns crisp & cheese melts. Serve hot.

# **Raisin Croissant Sandwich**

*Serves 4*

4 croissants or 4 burger buns
2 tbsp raisins (kishmish) - soaked in water for 10 minutes and strained
4 cheese slices
1 tbsp softened butter
1 capsicum - cut into half and then cut widthwise into very thin strips
a few cucumber slices - cut paper thin slices
a pinch of salt and ¼ tsp freshly crushed peppercorns
some tomato ketchup and mayonnaise to spread

**TO TOP**
a few olives, some lettuce or cabbage leaves

1.  Cut the croissants into 2 pieces. Spread the top piece with some tomato ketchup.
2.  Butter the lower piece of croissant. Sprinkle some raisins. Press a slice of cheese on it.
3.  Place 3-4 paper thin slices of cucumber on cheese slice. Arrange the capsicum strips on it. Sprinkle a pinch of salt and pepper. Squeeze or put drops of mayonnaise with a spoon on it.
4.  Press the other piece of croissant on top.
5.  Tear a small piece of cabbage or lettuce. Pass an olive through a toothpick and pierce the toothpick on the croissants through the leaf. Serve warm with some potato chips or fingers.

**Note:**   If croissants are not available, use soft dinner rolls or 8 plain slices of bread.

# Bread Tyres

*Serves 4*

6 slices of soft fresh bread
2 large potatoes - boiled and grated
1 onion - finely chopped
¼ cup finely chopped coriander
2 tbsp oil
½ tsp jeera (cumin seeds)
¼ tsp garam masala
¼ tsp haldi, ¾ tsp salt, ¼ tsp red chilli powder, ¼ tsp amchoor
1 tsp tomato ketchup

## SEALING PASTE
2 tsp cornflour or maida mixed with 2 tbsp water to make a paste

1. Heat oil. Add jeera and cook till golden. Add onions. Cook till onions turn transparent. Add salt, haldi, garam masala, red chilli powder and amchoor. Add the potatoes and coriander. Mix well. Add tomato ketchup. Keep filling aside.
2. Cut the sides of a slice, keep it flat on a rolling board.
3. Press, applying pressure with a rolling pin so that the holes of the bread close. Keep aside.
4. Similarly roll another slice.
5. Keep both the slices slightly overlapping at one end, about ¼" to get a long piece. Join the edges by applying some maida paste on the joint.
6. Spread a layer of the filling on the breads. Press the filling. Roll carefully.
7. Seal the end with maida paste.
8. Keep the roll, rolled up in a thin cloth for at least 10-15 minutes.
9. Deep fry each roll in hot oil till golden. Cut into 4 pieces and serve hot.

**Note:** If you do not want fried tyres, apply softened butter on the roll and cut into 3 pieces. Place upright in a greased oven proof glass dish and bake for 10 minutes at 200°C till light brown.

# Sprouty Peanut Sandwich

*Picture on facing page*          *Serves 2*

4 slices of bread - toasted in a toaster
½ cup moong sprouts (use ready-made or make at home)
1 tbsp butter, 4-6 flakes garlic - crushed, 1 onion - chopped
½ cup milk, ½ tsp sugar, ½ tsp lemon juice, ½ tsp soya sauce

### PEANUT PASTE

¼ cup roasted salted peanuts (moongphali), ½ tsp salt, ½ tsp red chilli powder
1 tsp dhania powder, 1 tsp jeera (cumin), 1 tbsp water

1. Grind all ingredients written under peanut paste in a mixer to a paste.
2. Heat butter in a kadhai. Add crushed garlic. Reduce heat, add onion and sprouts, cook till onion turns soft. Add peanut paste, mix.
3. Add milk, cook stirring on low heat for 3- 4 minutes, stirring constantly.
4. Add sugar, lemon juice and Soya sauce, stirring. Remove from fire. Keep aside for ½ hour.
5. Spread this mixture on 4 slices of toasted breads. Cut into 4 square or triangular pieces. Serve.

# Navrattan Sandwich

*Serves 3*      *Picture on opposite page*

6 slices of bread
3 tsp mint chutney (poodina chutney), see page 11 or tomato ketchup
3 tsp ready-made mayonnaise or see page 11
½ cup aloo bhujiya or navrattan mixture (Haldiram or any other)
1 potato - boiled and grated
1 small onion - chopped, ¼ tsp chaat masala

1. Take 3 slices of bread. Apply 1 tsp mint chutney or tomato ketchup on each of the 3 slices.

2. Take the other 3 slices and apply 1 tsp mayonnaise on each of them.
3. Mix Navrattan or bhujiya mixture, mashed boiled potatoes, chopped onion & chaat masala in a bowl.

4. Spread this mixture equally on all the three mayonnaise breads.
5. Cover it with chutney or ketchup bread slices. Cut diagonally. Serve with tomato ketchup.

# Apple Cinnamon Toast

*Serves 4-6*

2 large apples, 1 tbsp butter
juice of 1 lemon (2 tbsp), 1 tbsp honey
1 tsp powdered dalchini (cinnamon), ¼ tsp pepper
8 slices brown or white bread - toasted

1. Cut the apples into half without peeling and then again into half. Remove seeds. Cut each piece into thin slices.
2. Melt butter in a non stick pan and add apple slices, lemon juice, and honey. Cook on low flame for about 1-2 minutes, till apples get coated with butter. Sprinkle pepper and mix. Remove from heat. Keep aside.
3. Toast the bread slices lightly and lightly butter them.
4. Arrange some apple slices on the toast, to cover the toast almost completely. You may overlap the apple pieces.
5. Grate about ½ cube of cheese (2 tbsp) on the apples. Sprinkle a pinch of cinnamon powder and crushed peppercorns.
6. Heat oven to 210°C and put the toasts on the wire rack of the oven to grill the toasts for about 5 minutes. Serve.

# Russian Salad Sandwich

*Servings 4*

4 slices fresh bread
4 tbsp thick cream - approx.
½ cup thick curd (of full cream milk) - hang in a muslin cloth for ½ hour
1 carrot - grated
½ cup shredded cabbage
½ small kheera (cucumber) - grated
½ tsp mustard powder
¼ tsp each of powdered sugar & pepper, ¾ tsp salt

1. Hang curd in a muslin cloth for ½ hour.
2. Beat the hung curd well to make it smooth.
3. Except cream, add all other ingredients to the curd. Mix well.
4. Gradually mix in the cream, taking care not to thin down the mixture. Cool the mixture in the fridge for ½ hour.
5. Cut sides of bread. Apply paste on all slices. Join 2 slices. Cut into two triangular sandwiches. Serve.

# Vegetable Burger Sandwich

*This burger is just perfect for children and goes very well for adults too!*

*Picture on page 86*                    *Makes 6*

6 fresh ready-made burger buns
a few lettuce or cabbage leaves - remove hard stem & tear roughly into 1" pieces
6 cheese slices (optional)
a few slices of tomatoes (slice 1 medium tomato into 6 slices)
6 tbsp ready made mayonnaise

**BURGER (TIKKI)**
1 onion - finely chopped, 1 tbsp butter
2 small carrots - grated, 10-12 french beans - finely chopped
4 big potatoes - boiled & grated
1 bread slice - torn into pieces and churned in a mixer to get fresh bread crumbs
1 tsp salt or to taste, ½ tsp chilli powder, 1 tsp oregano, 1 tsp pepper
2 tbsp cheese spread or grated cheese or 4 tbsp grated paneer
1½ cup cornflakes - crushed to a rough powder or dry bread crumbs

1. Heat 3 tbsp butter in a kadhai. Add chopped onion & fry till transparent. Add carrots and beans. Stir fry for 5- 6 minutes. Add salt, chilli powder, oregano and pepper. Cook for 2-3 minutes. Mix boiled and grated potatoes. Cook for 7-8 minutes. Remove burger mixture from fire.
2. Add fresh bread crumbs prepared by grinding bread in the mixer to the burger mixture. Check seasonings. Make balls and shape into tikkis (burgers). Keep in the fridge till the time of serving.
3. Crush cornflakes roughly on a chakla belan or churn in a grinder just for a second. Do not make into a very fine powder. Spread the crushed cornflakes in a plate.
4. Sprinkle some water on the tikkis and immediately roll the wet tikkis on the crushed cornflakes or dry bread crumbs. Shallow fry in 2-3 tbsp oil in a non stick pan, till brown and crisp on both sides.
5. To assemble, cut buns into half. In a non stick pan or tawa press the buns till golden brown. Remove buns from pan.
6. Spread a few pieces of cabbage leaves. Put 1 cheese slice on top of it. Put a tomato slice on top of it. Put a hot tikki on the tomato slice. Sprinkle salt and pepper. Lastly, dot with 1 tbsp mayonnaise on the tikki. Place the half of the bun. Fix a tooth pick and serve hot.

# Open SANDWICH

## **Herbed Garlic Bread**

*Makes 15 slices*

4 tbsp softened butter
4 tbsp grated cheese
6 flakes of garlic - crushed
2 tbsp very finely chopped coriander or parsley
½ tsp black pepper corns - crushed or ½ tsp dried oregano
a french loaf - cut into ¼" thick slices

1. Beat butter in a bowl till smooth. Add cheese, garlic, coriander & oregano or pepper.
2. Diagonally cut slices of a french bread loaf (a long boat shaped loaf).
3. Spread with garlic butter.
4. Grill in a hot oven at 200°C for about 10 minutes, or till the edges and the bottom of the bread turns crisp.

# Grilled Veggie Sandwich

*Makes 4*

4 slices of bread, 1 capsicum - cut into 8 long pieces
1 zucchini (tori) - cut into thin long slices
4 big mushrooms - cut into slices
2 cheese cubes - peel with a peeler to get shavings, 4 green or black olives

### MARINADE
½ tsp oregano, ¼ tsp red chilli powder, ¼ tsp salt
2 tbsp olive oil, 1 tsp vinegar, one flake of garlic- crushed

1. Mix all ingredients of the marinade in a bowl. Add capsicum, tori and mushrooms.
2. Heat a pan on fire, add ½ of marinated veggies in a single layer. Cook till black patches appear on them. Keep them spread out while cooking.
3. Take a bread slice. Arrange 2 tori slices, 3-4 cheese shavings, 4 mushroom slices, 1 capsicum slice and 1 olive on each piece. Sprinkle salt & pepper. Repeat on other bread pieces with remaining vegetables.
4. Place on the wire rack of the oven (not tray) and bake at 180°C (350°F) for 15 minutes until golden and crisp. Serve hot.

# Spicy Grilled Buns

*Picture on facing page*              *Serves 4-5*

4 buns
2 cups baked beans (use tin)
1 tsp tabasco sauce, 1 tsp soya sauce
1 tbsp chilli garlic sauce, ¼ tsp pepper
1 green capsicum - chopped finely
2 tbsp chopped green coriander or parsley
2 cubes cheese - grated

1. Heat 2 tbsp butter in a pan, add the beans, add the three sauces and pepper. Remove from fire. Add capsicum and coriander.
2. Cut buns into halves horizontally and scoop out each piece of bun leaving a border of ½" all around.
3. Fill the buns with the bean mixture and top with grated cheese.
4. Grill in preheated oven for 4-5 minutes or till cheese melts. Dot with mustard sauce. Serve on a bed of lettuce.

# Tomato Canapes

*Makes a good cocktail snack for a party.*

*Makes 8 small pieces*

2 slices of bread - toasted in a toaster
1 spring onion - chop only the greens
1 cheese cube  - cut into 6 pieces

**PASTE**
1 tbsp chilli garlic sauce (maggi)
2 tbsp tomato ketchup, 1 tbsp curd, ¼ tsp soya sauce
¼ tsp oregano, ¼ tsp salt

1. Blend all ingredients of the paste in a small grinder till smooth.
2. Toast the bread slices in a toaster. Cut into 4 square pieces. Spread the tomato paste on each piece. Cover with greens of spring onion and top in the centre with a cheese cube. Sprinkle pepper. Serve immediately at room temperature.

◁ *Vegetable Burger Sandwich : Recipe on page 80*

# Baby corn Crostini

*Italian crostinis are small, thick toasts, topped with a variety of ingredients and cheese. These make wonderful starters.*

*Serves 6-8*

1 loaf french bread - cut into ½" thick slices
2 tsp garlic paste or finely chopped garlic
1 cup baby corns, cut into small pieces
½ tsp salt, ½ tsp pepper
¼ tsp oregano
2 tbsp oil
1 tomato - pureed in the mixer (½ cup)
some chilli flakes to sprinkle

**GARLIC BUTTER**
3 tbsp softened butter
4-5 flakes garlic - crushed
a pinch of salt & ¼ tsp freshly crushed peppercorns (saboot kali mirch)

## TOPPING
1 cup grated cheese, preferably parmesan or mozzarella
2 tbsp olive oil or any cooking oil, optional

1. Heat 2 tbsp oil. Reduce heat. Add garlic paste. Cook till it starts to change colour.
2. Add baby corns and stir fry till they change colour. Add salt, pepper, oregano and tomato puree. Cook covered till baby corns are tender and absolutely dry.
3. Prepare garlic butter by mixing softened butter with garlic, salt and pepper.
4. Cut French loaf diagonally into ½" thick slices.
5. On each slice spread some garlic butter. Sprinkle some chilli flakes.
6. Arrange a few baby corn pieces. Cover with grated cheese. Spoon a little olive oil on top.
7. Bake in a preheated oven for 10 minutes or till the base of the bread turns crisp and the cheese melts. Serve hot.

# Classic Pizzatini

*Serve tiny pizzas with different toppings.*

*Serves 6*

12 ready-made cocktail pizza bases
50 gms mozzarella or pizza cheese - grated

## TOMATO SPREAD
1 tbsp oil
4-5 flakes of garlic - crushed to a paste (1 tsp)
1/3 cup ready made tomato puree, 1 tbsp tomato sauce
½ tsp oregano (dried), ¼ tsp salt and 2 pinches pepper, or to taste

## ADD ONS
1 tbsp tinned sweet corn kernels or thinly sliced baby corns
1 mushroom - cut into paper thin slices
8-10 spinach leaves (paalak ke patte)
1 tbsp boiled peas (matar)
¼ of a green capsicum - finely chopped (1 tbsp diced)
salt and freshly ground peppercorns and oregano, to taste

1. To prepare the tomato spread, heat 1 tbsp oil. Reduce heat. Add garlic. Stir. Add tomato puree & tomato sauce, salt & pepper. Simmer for 3-4 minutes on low heat. Add oregano. Cook for 2 minutes till thick.
2. Boil 2 cups water with ½ tsp salt. Add spinach. Remove from fire after 1 minute. Strain and chop. Mix boiled peas with spinach.
3. Spread tomato spread on the pizza bases, leaving the edges clean. Sprinkle some cheese on the tomato spread, reserving some for top.
4. Put corn on 4 bases, mushrooms on the other 4 and blanched spinach and peas on the last 4 bases. Spread capsicum on the mushroom and corn pizzatinis. Sprinkle some salt and pepper. Sprinkle the remaining cheese on all of them. Sprinkle some oregano too on the cheese.
5. Place the pizzas on the wire rack of a hot oven (200°C). Grill for about 8-10 minutes till the base gets crisp and the cheese melts. To get a crisp pizza, oil the bottom of the base a little before grilling.
6. Serve them all together on a platter without cutting, along with some red chilli flakes & mustard sauce.

**Note :** To make mustard sauce, mix a little cream with some ready-made mustard paste to get the saucy consistency. To make chilli flakes, coarsely dry-grind the whole red chillies in a small spice grinder.

# Fruity Canapes

*Makes 10-12*

5-6 slices bread
1 small cucumber (kheera) - cut into thin slices without peeling
½ cup vinegar, 1 tsp sugar, 1 tsp salt
2 tbsp cheese spread
some bhuna jeera or crushed black pepper some chaat masala
1 orange, a few fresh or tinned cherry

1.  Put vinegar, sugar and salt in a bowl. Mix. Add cucumber and soak for 30 minutes in vinegar.
2.  Toast bread slices till crisp. Cut each slice into fancy shapes with a biscuit cutter or cut sides and then into 2 rectangles.
3.  Spread some cheese spread. Sprinkle some bhuna jeera or pepper.
4.  Place a pickled cucumber slice. Open an orange segment by cutting into half and place it on the side of kheera and top with a cherry.
5.  Sprinkle some chaat masala and serve.

LOW CAL.
Sandwiches

# Channa Chettinad Sandwich

*Picture on backcover*               *Serves 1- 2*

½ cup channas (safeed chhole) - soaked for 6-8 hours or overnight & boiled to get
1¼ cups boiled channas
4 bread slices
1 tbsp oil
1 onion - finely chopped, 10-12 curry leaves
1 tomato - deseeded and chopped
½ tsp salt, or to taste

### CHETTINAD MASALA (ROASTED & GROUND)
4 tbsp desiccated coconut (coconut powder)
½ tsp saboot dhania (coriander seeds)
¼ tsp jeera (cumin seeds), 1 tsp saunf (fennel)
1 dry, whole red chilli (sokhi lal mirch)
1 laung (clove), ½" dalchini (cinnamon stick)
seeds of 1 chhoti illaichi (green cardamom)

1. Heat a kadhai or tawa. Add coconut, saboot dhania, jeera, saunf, red chilli, laung, dalchini and seeds of chhoti illaichi. Stir-fry for 3-4 minutes till fragrant and golden. Remove from fire. Cool and grind to a smooth paste in a mixer with a little water.
2. Heat 1 tbsp oil in a pan, add the chettinad paste, cook for 2 minutes. Add onion, boiled channas, curry leaves, and salt. Mix well, mashing the channas for about 3-4 minutes. Add tomatoes, mix.
3. Spread some mashed channa mixture on one piece of bread. Place the other piece on it. Press well.
4. Grill in a sandwich toaster or in a pan till golden brown and crisp.
5. Cut into 2 pieces and serve hot. Repeat with the other 2 slices.

**Note:** You can do this with any leftover channa mixture also.

# Mushroom Croustades

*Picture on page 2*                    *Serves 2*

2 hot dog buns

**FILLING**

9-10 mushrooms (120 gms) - chopped finely, 1 tbsp butter
2 small spring onions - chopped till the greens
2 tsp veg oyster sauce or soya sauce, ½ tsp salt, ½ tsp pepper or to taste

1. Cut one hot dog bun into half lengthwise. Scoop out the soft center portion with a knife, leaving a border. Cut both the pieces further into 2 pieces.
2. Grill all the 4 pieces in a preheated oven till crisp.
3. For the filling, heat butter in a pan, add white of spring onions. Cook till golden. Add mushrooms, cook for 3-4 minutes or till dry.
4. Add soya sauce, salt and pepper. Add greens of spring onion. Mix. Remove from fire.
5. Spoon this mixture into grilled hollowed bread croustades and serve.

# Diet Cole Slaw Sandwich

*Makes 2*

2 slices of brown bread

**DIET COLE SLAW**
4 tbsp grated cabbage
4 tbsp thickly grated carrot (use the biggest holes of your grater to grate)
1 tsp tomato sauce
¼ tsp salt and pepper, or to taste, ½ tbsp mustard paste
½ tbsp vinegar, a pinch of sugar
2 tbsp chopped capsicum - chopped very finely
3 tbsp curd

1.  Grate cabbage and carrot. Chop capsicum pieces finely.
2.  Mix all ingredients of diet cole slaw in a bowl.
3.  Spread mixture on a plain slice. Place the other slice on it. Press lightly.
4.  Serve as it is or toast in a equity toaster till crisp and golden brown.
    Cut into 2 pieces and serve.

# Slimmers Choice Sandwich

*Serves 4*

2 slices brown bread
some lettuce leaves

**SPREAD**
2 tbsp paneer, 2 tbsp milk, ¼ tsp coffee
1 tbsp basil or coriander
¼ tsp salt and pepper, or to taste, some red chilli flakes
1 tbsp chopped tomato

1. Wash the lettuce leaves.
2. Grind all the ingredients of spread into a smooth paste.
3. Spread mixture on a plain slice.
4. Arrange a lettuce leaf on top of it and place the other slice on it. Press lightly.
5. Cut into 2 triangular pieces. Repeat with the other slices.

# Grilled Curd Cheese Fingers

*Serves 4-5*

1 cup thick curd (prepared from toned milk) - hang for 1-2 hours
3-4 tbsp cabbage - shredded, 2-3 tbsp carrot - grated
1 green chilli - deseeded and finely chopped
salt and pepper to taste
2 tbsp green mint or coriander chutney (optional), see page 11
6 slices bread, preferably brown bread

1. Beat hung curd in a bowl till smooth.
2. Add cabbage, carrot, green chilli, salt and pepper. Mix well. Add a little extra salt, otherwise the fingers taste bland.
3. Spread the curd mix generously on a slice.
4. Spread some chutney on another slice. Place the chutney slice, with the chutney side down on the curd slice. Press well.
5. Grill in a sandwich toaster or in the oven on the wire rack till browned.
6. Cut into 4 fingers and serve hot. Repeat with the other 4 slices.

# Curry Patta Toasties

*Serves 4*

75 gm paneer - crumbled or mashed roughly (¾ cup), 2 tbsp suji (semolina)
½ tsp salt, or to taste, ¼ tsp pepper, or to taste, ½ onion - very finely chopped
½ tomato - cut into half deseeded and chopped finely
2 tbsp curry leaves, 3 bread slices - toasted
¼ - ½ tsp rai (small brown mustard seeds), 3 tsp oil

1. Mix the suji, salt and pepper with the paneer using your fingers.
2. Add the onion, tomato and curry leaves.
3. Spread this mixture carefully on the toasted bread slices, keeping the edges neat.
4. Sprinkle some rai over the mixture, pressing down carefully with your finger tips.
5. Heat 1 tsp oil in a pan. Add a slice of bread with the topping side down.
6. Cook until it turns golden brown and crisp. Add a little more oil for the next slice if required. Cut into 8 triangular pieces and serve hot.

# Some Sandwich Accompaniments

## French Fries

1. Peel 2-3 potatoes and cut into ¼" thick round slices. Stack the slices and cut them into ¼" broad strips or fingers.
2. Keep for about 10 minutes in cold water to which 1-2 tsp salt and 1 tbsp lemon juice has been added.
3. Drain and wipe dry on a clean kitchen towel.
4. Sprinkle 1 tsp of maida on the potato fingers to absorb any water if present. Mix well with fingers.
5. Heat oil in a kadhai, about half kadhai full or slightly less than half full.
6. Add all the fingers and fry for 3-4 minutes till very light golden. Remove from oil on a paper napkin. Immediately sprinkle ¼ tsp salt.
7. Just before serving, reheat the oil and fry the chips quickly for 2 minutes until crisp and golden brown.

# Glazed Vegetables

*Serves 4*

1 tbsp butter, 1 tsp sugar, 3-4 cherry tomatoes, 3-4 French beans - cut into 2" pieces
4- 5 small florets of cauliflower or broccoli, 1 carrot - diagonally cut into slices
a few drops Tabasco sauce (optional), ½ tsp pepper and salt to taste

1.  For the glazed vegetables, boil 4-5 cups water with 1 tsp salt. Add vegetables except tomatoes. As soon as the boil returns, remove from fire and strain. Refresh in cold water. Keep aside.
2.  At the time of serving- heat butter in a pan with sugar. Stir, add vegetables, tomatoes and Tabasco sauce. Mix well for 3-4 minutes to coat vegetables with butter. Sprinkle pepper and salt to taste.

# Pickled Cucumber

*Serves 4*

### MIX TOGETHER IN A BOWL & KEEP ASIDE FOR 10 MINUTES

1 kheera (cucumber) - peeled and scraped with a peeler to get paper thin long pieces
1 thick green chilli - deseeded and chopped, ¼ cup white vinegar, ¼ cup warm water
1 tsp salt, 1 tsp sugar

1.  Mix all ingredients written under mix together. Strain after 15 minutes.

*Romance : Recipe on page 60* ➤

# Nita Mehta's BEST SELLERS (Vegetarian)

**Taste of DELHI**

**NEW MICROWAVE**

**MEXICAN Vegetarian**

**Taste of PUNJAB**

**JHATPAT Khaana**

**CONTINENTAL Vegetarian**

**Eggless Desserts**

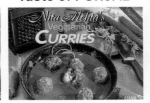

**Vegetarian CURRIES**

**Eggless OVEN Recipes**

**Food for Children**

**Different ways with CHAAWAL**

**Different ways with VEGETABLES**